WELCOME TO

YORK, they say, is the city that never changes. That is the cosy perception of a world constantly swept away and renewed, but far more comforting is the truth.

Namely that York, as everywhere else, is constantly evolving. What remains unchanged, however, are its values.

Generations of city fathers have been guided not just by common sense in finding the balance between heritage and the here-and-now, but also by a sort of ancestral memory.

Just as important as keeping faith with generations past in the ancient capital is keeping faith with generations of the future.

Buildings do not a city make. It is the people who are all important, and the buildings merely reflect their diligence, glory and sometimes carelessness.

For that reason no city has been, could, or should be preserved in aspic.

The Yorkshire Evening Press, 114 years old, exists to reflect that change and sometimes to participate in it.

With the help of our own extensive

One of the earliest photographs of York - Kings Staith - taken by photographic pioneer William Henry Fox Talbot in 1845. In the following pages we chart the changing face of the city from the early days of photography to the present day.

photographic archives, and those of eminent local historians we look at Then and Now. We compare the way it was in Victorian, Edwardian, between the wars and post war times, with the way it is now. And revel in spotting the difference.

CREDITS

Words and research: Ron Godfrey
Design and layout: Martin Lacy
With special thanks to Hugh Murray (see page 96)

One of the earliest photographs taken by Fox Talbot in July, 1845, of Museum Street looking towards a partly obscured Minster. When Dean Augustus Duncombe came to York in 1858 he led a campaign to demolish the obstructions.

The Dean got his way. Now the west front of the Minster is in full view bar trees which line Duncombe Place, the new street named in his honour. It was closed to through traffic when Deangate was shut, creating a cathedral close.

FACING PAGE: Bootham in 1880 photographed from Bootham Bar. Opposite the lamp post (beyond which a man leans angularly) is The White Horse pub which was rebuilt in 1892. The sign points the way to the School for the Blind, now no longer in York. Note the narrow road where the blurred boy on the right is standing. That was the entrance to Gillygate widened in 1907 to accommodate electric trams. Note the sign behind the lamp post on the right pointing to the Skating Rink. It was later demolished to make way for the Salvation Army's citadel in York.

RIGHT: the junction has become one of York's worst bottlenecks for traffic as cars wait in line on the approach roads. Otherwise the roofline is much the same (and the White Horse public house still gallops into the future but in a newer building erected in 1894).

St Helen's Square, 1873, photographed by Francis Frith. On the left is the ornate Georgian window of the shop then occupied by Stephen Davis, furrier, soon to be taken over by Joseph Terry, who bought into what was to become the York-based sweet empire. Mr Terry's original shop was just off-picture next door and he expanded into the Davis premises. Opposite was Mrs M.Magean's Irish Linen Warehouse which she occupied until 1880.

The building next to the church had its top storey removed in the 1930s after it was considered unsafe. It was that way when Bernard Thorpe and Partners occupied the premises in the late 1950s. Later, cobbles were restored and cars restricted. Mrs Magean's old premises were pulled down in 1929 to turn what was a triangle into a square (and also gave the Lord Mayor a pleasant breakfast-time view of St Helen's Church from the Mansion House dining room).

Jubbergate, 1880, two pictures taken by photographer Joseph Duncan and spliced together but slightly out of synchronisation due to a trick of perspective. (Note the mismatching window in Newgate.) It features A Wells, the house clearers and part of Cook's shoeshop next door (with J Dalby, outfitters and specialists in boots and shoes as round-the-corner rivals). On the corner is the Ebor Eating House.

History decreed a kind of musical chairs in this corner of the city. Wells and Cook are no more, but the site, after drastic restoration in 1927, was a succession of establishments devoted to food - a tea room, cafe, restaurant or, as is the case now, a fine delicatessen and restaurant. Ebor Eating House is barely a memory as is the shoe specialist J.Dalby, but one of the 280 branches of Timpson shoe repairers is carrying on the footwear tradition of this area very nicely, thank you.

FACING PAGE: Boatyard on the downstream side of the Ouse in October, 1854, photographed by Roger Fenton (who, by covering action in the Crimea, became the first famous cameraman war correspondent). Where the man with the topper - the boat owner perhaps? - is standing equates roughly with where Lendal Bridge was to be opened nine years later. Fenton must have positioned himself on a balcony under the waterworks tower.

RIGHT: The little fishing and cargo boats are replaced by part of the fleet of the pleasure cruise company, the White Rose Line. The Viking Hotel seems to have sprouted from nowhere and the little tree just before the white castellated Guildhall which marked where a new York Council chamber was built in 1892 has flourished magnificently.

Just inside Micklegate Bar in 1852, recorded by William Pumphrey. The building jutting out on the right is the Jolly Bacchus pub. Earliest reference to it is in 1787.

The Jolly Bacchus has vanished. Its closure in 1873 to widen the bar lane meant its licence being transferred to the Melbourne in Cemetery Road. It also meant that a fourth arch was exposed to view for all the world to marvel at.

FACING PAGE: One of the earliest photos ever taken of the Ouseside in 1852 by William Pumphrey - but where exactly is it? We are certain it is near to the future site of Skeldergate Bridge, but is it downstream of Kings Staith on the north bank or Queens Staith on the south? The answer might lie in the cupola glimpsed on the skyline, but perhaps distorted by an ancient camera lens.

ABOVE: Gone are buildings on the right - warehouses mainly - but is the house on the left the same one - albeit altered and extended? And then there is that cupola. Close examination reveals it to be the same - or an exact copy - as the one in the earlier picture. And the cupola in the modern picture sits atop part of York's Castle Museum - the section that once formed part of York Prison - which is on the south side of the river behind Kings Staith.

First Salvation Army meeting ever in York, in St Sampson's Square in 1881. But not everyone took the blood and fire flag seriously. Some scalliwags saw the soul-saving outside the Golden Lion as a cue for troublemaking. The newspapers later described the meeting as "disgraceful and a burlesque, more likely to promote wickedness than the will of God."

A much less frenetic scene. The three medieval buildings on the left of the 1881 picture were replaced in 1900 with what is now Brown's Corner, while the Golden Lion's position equates exactly with the department store's tea shop. The view of that side of the Square is now obscured by trees, the lavatories for the disabled, and an occasional ice cream trailer.

FACING PAGE: Shambles, 1873 by photographer Francis Frith, depicting it as history intended - namely a street of butchers. Its name in medieval times was "The Flesh Shambles," derived from the Middle English word-shammel, meaning bench. A year before this picture was taken there were 39 shopkeepers recorded there, of whom 25 were butchers.

THIS PAGE: There is a hairdresser, a tea shop, the quaint and the cute, but not a butcher in sight. The last of them, Dewhurst, left in 1993.

Clifford's Tower, 1852, dwarfed by the castellated governor's house of York prison, a structure eventually demolished in 1935. In the background is the elegant never-changing spire of St Mary's church, Castlegate.

In the background is the Stakis hotel. The monstrous white building was bought by the city authorities, who intended to use the site for new council offices. World War Two intervened. Then the money ran out and the site became a car park.

Pavement in 1845, featuring the beautiful dome of St Crux above a concave line of three storey buildings.
Take a closer look at the buildings on the right. They include The York Herald office - home of the newspaper which was a forerunner of The Yorkshire Evening Press.

The sight line of buildings is convex and gone is the St Crux church and tower, dynamited in 1887 when found to be unsafe. The range of jettied buildings including the York Herald office, was demolished to make way for trams proceeding down Coppergate to turn into Piccadilly.

York railway station at the turn of the century. A train is due any moment. You can tell by the postures of expectation of the bowler-hatted passengers, by the brass-buttoned porters who wait in readiness and by the two milkchurns which have been strategically placed for loading aboard.

The sense of expectancy has gone as people mill about before their train is due. Between the pillars - fewer than of old - are electronic monitors. What was the ladies room first class is now a waiting room. The single tracks are all that is left of the cat's cradle of rails in this age where the car is king. Many tracks were taken out during electrification.

Goodramgate, pictured in 1902. The archway next door to J Todd, grocer and tea dealer, leads to College Street. On the other side of the alleyway was John Wharton's glass and china shop - and opticians!

Those Jacobean-style buildings were torn down to make way for the new Deangate to burst through a year after our historic picture was taken. One consolation is that you now have a clear view of the Tudor frontage of what was J Todd grocers.

Parliament Street, York, photographed between 1902 and 1906 looking towards Pavement and Piccadilly. Isaac Walton's tailors arrived in 1902. At the far end is Braimes, the Tadcaster brewers and next door is what was the Saturday office of Isaac Poad & Sons, corn and potato merchants - handy for the Saturday corn market which used to be held at the bottom of Coppergate. Poad, now based at Cattal, near Wetherby, used to have its head office on part of the site now occupied by The Yorkshire Evening Press in Walmgate, where the staff restaurant still bears its name.

Where once stood Braimes and Isaac Poad & Sons is blotted out by the fondly named "Splash Palace," the recently-built town centre office with public toilet facilities below. Let it be known, though, that the buildings which housed the two firms went in the link up between Parliament Street and Piccadilly. Half of the arched-windowed building was occupied on the ground floor, until recently, by Currys electrical store which has now moved to Clifton Moor trading estate. The other half of that elegant structure was demolished in 1961 to make way for the modern building that is now Marks & Spencer.

College Street, around 1902 - the view on the other side of the Goodramgate picture on Page 26. The entire area to the right of the arch was destined for demolition in the quest to extend Deangate.

The breakthrough is complete. The area in front of St Williams College off picture is busier. This is the age of Continental Britain and of people-watching from boulevard tables...

Turn-of-the-century view of Low Petergate, taken from the crossroads with Church Street. More than just a charming place showing a pretty face to tourists, it has always been a working street. (Beales Brush and Mat Warehouse says it all.) On the right, near those wonderful gas lamps, was Merriman, the city's famous pawnbroker's shop.

The medieval geometry of the rooftops has remained but the right hand side has been wiped out and replaced with monuments to modernity of the kind that some argue are symbols of the architectural follies of the philistine 1960s. By the way the sign of the hanging brush over Beales is on display in the Castle Museum.

Coney Street between 1900 and 1910. It was an exciting shopping street then, too. You could have a quick browse as you ambled by on horse and cart. On the left are two shopfronts of Leak and Thorpe, York's first department store. It opened in Parliament Street in 1848 and in 1869 moved to Coney Street. A mysterious fire broke out in its gentleman's outfitting department while closed on January 23, 1933. The building had to be demolished.

Busier than ever, but now traffic is restricted and through most of the day pedestrians reign on the newly-paved footstreet. Where Leak and Thorpe once stood is now a moulded edifice in concrete occupied by the Next chain store. But your eye is still drawn to that eye-catching attraction, the Little Admiral's clock, attached to St Martin Le Grand church. It took a 1942 air raid bomb to dislodge the ornate timepiece. But all was restored by 1968.

Inside the machine shop at York Carriageworks in 1910 - one of an intriguing collection of pictures held by the National Railway Museum. This forest of flying drive belts powered possibly by steam would be a modern-day factory inspector's nightmare. Here, it seems, was where dozens were employed to make small metal fittings from raw material for the building and repair of rolling stock. Although carriages and wagons were made of wood they had steel underframes riveted together. Despite the clack-crack-crash of the whiplashing leather drive belts, no one wore ear protectors then.

Where have all the people gone? The same workshop at ABB Engineering Ltd. The Swiss-Swedish firm bought Brel, itself the privatised successor to British Rail Engineering Ltd, and has since made a succession of job cuts. Here it takes relatively few people amid the quietly humming machinery to build sections of the bodyshell for the new Eurotram bound for Strasbourg. Where 84 years ago, manufacturing began from scratch, now parts are originated elsewhere and assembly is the name of the game. This workshop in Holgate Road is also used as a storeroom.

The 1908 Ebor meeting. It's fancy net hats and bowlers on the York racecourse looking towards Knavesmire Gates. The course is on the left and the crowd in the distance mills about where the parade ring is now.

The open grass lawn has gone, to be replaced by the parade ring, pre-race saddling boxes and tiered seats. And the saplings in the old picture have grown up to provide shade and enhance the scene.

A sweet view from Lendal Bridge in 1903... of the old Rowntree factory before it moved to Haxby Road. Henry Isaac Rowntree started business in Coppergate in 1862. Two years later he bought an iron foundry, several cottages and a tavern in Tanner Row and Wellington Row, where he established his factory.

New giants have taken their place - in the shape of the General Accident building and, in the distance, the Viking Hotel, while banking of the river bank has confined the Ouse and citizens now have a pleasant garden to sit in where once the scenery was definitely industrial.

Sold, for £1,500 - that was how much St William's College fetched in a private sale by its then owner, Frank Green, in 1902 - three years before the postcard featuring this picture of it was used. Built in 1461 as a residence for the college of chantry priests serving York Minster, it was later used as a printing house by Charles I. By the 19th century it was divided into tenements and bought by Mr Green who converted it into a single building again before selling it for the sum he paid for it.

St William's College has been restored to its former glory, thanks to a massive restoration appeal
in 1983 by the Archbishop of York, Dr John Habgood. The appeal, backed by the York Civic Trust, helped to raise the more
than £300,000 necessary at the time to restore and redevelop it. Now the building, which boasts an award-winning
restaurant and tearooms, is popular with residents and tourists alike.

FACING PAGE: Ah, what excitement this building brought to York - and within it how many romances were forged? It is The Electric Cinema, Fossgate, the city's first purpose-built cinema, photographed shortly after its opening in 1911. Unlike other cinemas where the projector was in the ticket box, The Electric - later given the upmarket moniker of The Scala - ensured that the highly inflammable celluloid was kept separate from viewers in a special projection room at the back. Alas, for all its safety consciousness, and its namechange, it became just another victim of television and closed in April, 1957.

THIS PAGE: Gone are the ticket kiosks. And in their place is the showroom of Macdonalds furniture store into which the store expanded from next door. With the cinema's theatrical Doultonware gable and lionmask frieze still perfectly preserved, it must be one of the most unusual furniture stores in Britain.

Davygate, around 1903. On the left is a building erected in 1881 by CJ Melrose for his wine and spirit business. On the right is the aptly-named tailor's shop called R.Cutter. Note the horse and cart.

No, the horse and cart has not taken more than 90 years to reach the corner! On the left it's goodbye to Mr Melrose's architectural monument and hello to the Davygate Centre, an arcade completed in 1968. On the right, R.Cutter, tailors, is no more. Now it is part of Brown's department store and the area is known colloquially as Brown's Corner.

A postman hauls his delivery cart alongside horse and tram tracks in Nessgate circa 1900. On the right is St Michael's, Spurriergate. The gabled building in the centre was the Star and Garter, of which there is a mention in the history books of 1749. On the far corner is another pub, the Coach and Horses. Most of these Georgian buildings had medieval timber frames.

Gone! All those buildings on the left were demolished in 1907 for street-widening to accommodate electric trams. Now the building there is a single, relatively modern block, once the home of a much larger Coach and Horses pub (known locally as the 'Big Coach'). The block now houses Thomas Cook and the Royal Bank of Scotland.

A postcard sent in 1919 featuring the view down Water End to Clifton Ferry (the rowing boat in the foreground?) years before the arrival of a permanent Clifton Bridge. There is a sweet, tree-shaded walkway to the river's edge and the Ouse laps the end of the slipway. On the far bank on the right is the ferry's landing stage on the Leeman Road side of the river.

The stepped wall is still there but gone are the raised pedestrian walkway and hand rails. Now the bridge - built in 1963 - dominates. It came after a Bailey Bridge was experimentally built, timed to divert traffic from the city centre wedding procession of the Duke of Kent and Katherine Worsley on June 8, 1961.

Layerthorpe Postern, 1920. Hunts brewery in Aldwark inside the city walls dominates the view. On the left is the building housing a store and workshop for the former York firm of painters and decorators, Bellerby's.

The brewery and the terraced houses were demolished in 1972. Now a Sainsbury's car park dominates the skyline. Still there is the old workshop - although Bellerby's has now gone .

Micklegate, 1931, featuring St John's Church, now York Arts Centre, but for a time the Architectural Institute, precursor of York University. It had magnificent wrought iron railing. The photo was taken to support the campaign by the then Archbishop of York, William Temple, to demolish the redundant church. He failed.

Gone are the railings to allow for the widening of the road - and, for the same reason, gone are those wonderful Victorian houses on the right, making way for the more modern structure of Victoria House. But the church building, whose north aisle is associated with a chantry founded in 1320, lives on.

Goodramgate, photographed in 1916 towards the junction with Petergate. Note the gas holder on the extreme left. They were placed outside to illuminate shop windows at night. Inside the premises was thought to be too dangerous. Note also the exposed timbered beams of the 14th century Lady Row on the right.

New fashion has guided the architectural style of the 1990s and the exposed beams have been replaced by rendered
buildings on the same Lady Row. That, and the 1960s concrete arcade on the left, are
among few changes wrought by time.

Blossom Street, 1927, ten years before the Odeon cinema was built on the site. The land was the garden of the house which in this picture was partly occupied by the Crescent Cafe but was grand enough to have a famous occupant. Feilden Thorp, headmaster of Bootham School, moved out of the school and into the house in 1875.

Look what blossomed in Blossom Street - and it is still attracting cinemagoers after 57 years. The Odeon was one of many throughout Britain of similar architectural style commissioned by Oscar Deutsch. The name Odeon was taken not just from the Greek for theatre but also chosen for its acronym, Oscar Deutsch Entertains Our Nation.

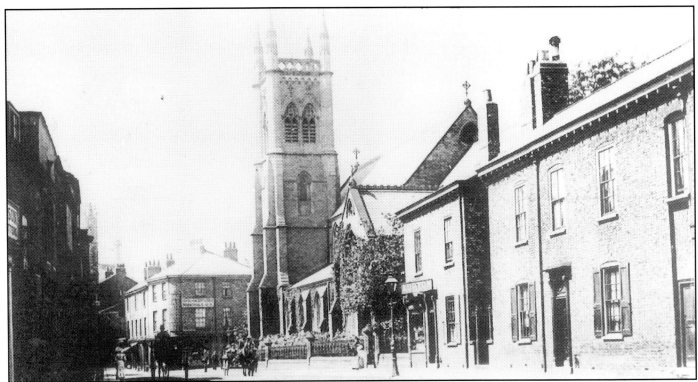

This proud church once stood in Monkgate, as this picture looking towards Monk Bar and taken c.1920 shows. It is St Maurice's on the corner of Monkgate and Lord Mayor's Walk. Built in 1878 to replace a much smaller church, it was demolished in 1967.

Gone are the terraced houses on the right, replaced by a faceless modern building. Where St Maurice's once stood is a green and graveyard. Straight ahead is Bulmers Corner. More than 70 years ago it was occupied by a chemist whose bronchial linctus came highly recommended. Now it is an antiques and clearance business.

Gale Lane, Acomb, looking towards Front Street in about 1923. On the right is a working farm; on the left agricultural cottages. The road used to go no further than the former Common Moor, Acomb Knoll and to the kennels of the York and Ainsty Hunt.

After the Second World War every dwelling bar the one at the end of
Gale Lane was swept away and ultimately replaced with
new suburbia. The road now links with Dringhouses.

The new consumer society of 1930 shouts from hoardings on the wall of a building on the corner of Clarence Street and Union Terrace. They preach a materialist message which sits uncomfortably next to the adjoining Methodist chapel.

Images of Oxo, Symingtons Coffee and Pioneer matches have vanished into oblivion - along with many of the buildings in this row that once stretched down to the junction with Lord Mayor's Walk, demolished to provide a car park.

Queens Staith, 1925 - and more signs of the acquisitive era to come. One look at this scene and you were bound to dash home, light up a Player's and glug down Camp's coffee or Bovril (which gives strength to win!).

Alas! The hoardings have gone and apart from the building alongside the Ouse Bridge stairs, the two structures without their hoardings look faded and jaded, with pigeons roosting in the roof of one of them.

An ordinary street scene at the three way junction of Acomb Road, Poppleton Road and Holgate Road in what is believed to be around 1931 (the roller blind on the top rather than the bottom deck of the tram dates it beyond 1928). The tram shelter was built for the council in 1914 by contractor Joseph Hodsman for £156.5s. The telephone kiosk was of the white concrete type introduced by the GPO in 1922, later to be replaced by the famous red boxes.

The grocer's shop, formerly hidden behind the tram shelter has become a Spar shop and is clearly visible,
the tram shelter has naturally vanished along with the phone and the street furniture and design
has changed utterly with the advent of traffic lights controlling the junction.
That tree in the distance still flourishes.

The Grand cinema and ballroom entrance in Clarence Street not long after it opened in 1919. It was York's third purpose-built cinema. Patrons arriving and leaving the building were left in no doubt about what was sold in the shop next door! It was also designed to catch the attention of passengers in passing trams.

The Grand closed in 1958 and was a car showroom before being demolished in 1989, and along with it the entire row of houses, including Kirk's wine and spirits. Object - to clear the way for the Clarence Street car park.

The Davy Hall Restaurant, Davygate, c.1929. Built by George Edwin Barton in 1904 it was designed by architects Penty and Penty in distinctive art nouveau style and with a much-talked-about stained glass canopy.

The restaurant is part of Browns department store, which has gradually grown to include buildings both along Davygate and in St Sampson's Square - an area that has come to be known as Brown's corner.

George Howson, known as wrap-it-up George, set up his York fish stall at Davygate Corner twice a week in the 1920s stocking it with the produce of his Hull trawler. It was a muddy place then but perfectly positioned for a trawl of shoppers lured to the sale at Brown's department store.

Against a background of changed facades, including the Davygate Centre and a new disabled toilet and payphone shelter, the area is paved and more comfortable to stroll on - but with not a stall in sight.

The junction of Rougier Street, Tanner's Moat and Station Rise, 1931, with railway offices in the background. The Evening Press was prominently displayed on the wall of Lumbs newsagents and tobacconist. The traffic lights are particularly significant. They were among the first to be installed in York.

Taken from the same position in Tanner's Moat there is nothing left
of the old view, apart from the shop on the corner of Tanner's Moat - then a fruit shop, now a florists.
The new view is dominated by the General Accident Life Assurance building.

FACING PAGE: Holgate Mill on Windmill Rise around 1920 - in the days when unusually it had five sails, rather than four or six. Built in 1792 by George Waud the five sail technology was introduced by John Smeaton - who built the Eddystone lighthouse off the Isle of Wight. A steam engine fitted at the end of the 19th century helped the mill to grind corn on windless days. When gales irreparably damaged the sails in January 1930 electric power took over until milling ceased in 1938. There is a controversial claim that the mill actually derived from a medieval corn mill on the site.

THIS PAGE: It is a grade II listed building which stands as a giant monument to the great days of windmills - at one time York was surrounded by 20 of them. It was part of an estate owned by Mrs Eliza Gutch who willed that Holgate Lodge should be demolished and the remainder of the estate near the mill should be built upon with homes. Now the windmill, which stands in glorious isolation on a traffic island, is unlikely ever to have sails fitted again, if only because they might damage rooftops!

Stubbs ironmongers, Foss Bridge House, Fossgate, 1926. It is 90 years since Francis Richard Stubbs was made redundant from Robert Varvill's ironmongery shop for which part settlement was a pony, named Maggie. After travelling with Maggie as an ironmonger salesman, he ultimately set up shop in Lady Peckitt's Yard; shortly after his death in 1915 the firm moved into Fossgate, finding a winning formula for display of goods which holds true today. The 1926 staff are clearly proud of their window within which are festooned hanging pails and piping, ladders and latticework, Baxi fires and brooms

Only the staff has changed along with the nature of the products - though not the what-you-see-hanging is what you get style of window dressing. And phooey to neon. If the double faceted wooden nameplate and gilt frontispiece were good enough for the Stubbs forefathers they are good enough for their progeny and for visitors who stroll in to absorb the atmosphere and walk out with a hoe and nails they never realised they needed.

Hear the tinkle of recent history? Work takes place in 1927 on extending the underground gents' loo which was first excavated in Parliament Street in 1894.

What a relief...the facilities are much more palatial. The building on the corner, now Barclays, is as beautiful as ever, but it has been cropped of its cupola and gothic gabled windows on the top floor where modernity has taken hold.

Whip-Ma-Whop-Ma-Gate around 1946. Can it really be that double decker Service No.6 buses wound their way down St Saviourgate? Can it also really be that this narrow slalom was a two-way street? Seeing is believing: Behind the turning bus is another heading the other way. The family footwear shop advertising Joyway shoes had a sale on but it couldn't save the shop from closure.

It is still a grassy - but now much more leafy - corner. (Could that tiny tree of nearly 50 years ago be the same tall creature outside the church hall?). The shoeshop is gone, with the entire block demolished to make way for an area now occupied by Stonebow House, with the Halifax Building Society at its closest end. The Victorian building on the other side of St Saviourgate survives still, now much more obvious in all its elegance and occupied by Harrowell Shaftoe, solicitors.

On the verge of change. View in 1968 from the top of the Yorkshire Insurance Company offices in Rougier Street. Plans were afoot for a central bus station for York. To the right of the Pageant and County hotels is the former Bushells site in Tanner Row. The property ran back to the unoccupied building with large windows, linking up with the two Railway Street properties formerly occupied by printers De Little & Fenwick's and Dick's.

Change has come. From the same perspective in what is now the General Accident building you can see the flat rooftop of that proposed bus station, now an extension of the General Accident building. It obstructs the view of Tanner Row. A supermarket and car park now fit snugly into part of the area behind what was the County Hotel. But the George Hudson Street (formerly Railway Street) curve of buildings on the other side of the road is as pleasant a sight as ever.

St Andrewgate from Kings Square in July, 1969 - regarded as an eyesore with cars littering the side of what was little more than an alley in a part of York where commercial interests rather than residents ruled. A report by international architect Lord Esher called for action to lure people back to live within the city walls.

St Andrewgate is smarter and lived in with a series of housing developments; double yellow lines ward off cars and vans, while parking facilities have been made available for cycles. Wood & Richardson's printing premises now house a discount store, while the Goodramgate firm of sports outfitter Newitts has expanded through to a smart new building on the corner.

1965, showing Forsselius' garage in Blossom Street and its controversial petrol pumps - the first in York. The company's planning application for the pumps was rejected in 1920. But the next year with the backing of the powerful Anglo American Oil Company consent was granted and the devices were installed in September 1921.

Where once Forsselius stood is now Hein Gericke, the motorcycle
clothing shop while the Lion and Lamb, later the Nickel and Dime, is
a pub no more. Otherwise not much is different - apart from the volume of traffic.

October, 1955, crowds gather to watch Ald Fred Brown, Lord Mayor of York, open the new Stonebow highway. The widening to 50ft meant cutting out two dangerous corners and the narrow roadway of St Saviourgate. Cost: £22,000 - the first major development undertaken by the council since the creation of Piccadilly more than 40 years earlier.

It did the trick, though nobody back in 1955 predicted speed humps. The gaunt monstrosity behind the Mayor is now gone - replaced by the sleek, neat pub, The Northern Wall (previously known as The Board, The Stonebow and The Boulevard). Otherwise not much has altered except what constitutes a public sense of occasion...

FACING PAGE: Bridging the gap. Work in progress on a new bridge spanning Tang Hall Beck between Stray Road and Applecroft Road in February, 1968.

THIS PAGE: This link between Burnholme and Stockton Lane areas of York hardly merits a blink from most motorists crossing the bridge in Stray Road. Some are unaware that there is a beck to be crossed at all.

The Historian

A MAJOR contributor to Then and Now is York historian Hugh Murray of Burtonstone Lane. Ironically this 62-year-old author, whose Graveyard Guide of York is the latest of 13 of his definitive works about the city, was born in Hull.

It was only by the time he was 11 years old that his railwayman father who moved around the country on the promotional ladder, settled in York and the young Hugh who had been to six different schools settled for the first time in his life.

On leaving St Peter's School, where he showed more interest in science than history, he read physics at Oxford, then became a graduate signal engineer for British Rail, interrupted by two years national service as officer in command of workshops at RAF Honington, Suffolk.

Returning to his railway career, he eventually became divisional engineer for East Anglia and his fascination with the history of Norwich was transferred to York when he moved back to the city to take up his post as divisional engineer for Leeds.

He later took charge of maintenance of signals throughout Eastern region and retired early in 1988, since when his

York historian Hugh Murray: a passion for the history of York

passion for the history of York has manifested itself in numerous tracts, articles and books, his first being The Horse Tramways of York.

Other Hugh Murray titles include Heraldry and the Buildings of York, Whittock's Bird's Eye View of York and York Through the Eyes of the Artist.